THE
NATURAL
HUSTLE

BOOKS BY EVA H.D.

The Natural Hustle

EVA H.D.

McClelland & Stewart

McClelland & Stewart and colophon are registered trademarks of Penguin Random House Canada Limited.

Published simultaneously in the United States of America.

Library and Archives Canada Cataloguing in Publication data is available upon request.

ISBN: 978-0-7710-0467-4
ebook ISBN: 978-0-7710-0468-1

Book design by Talia Abramson
Cover image: Jac Martinez
Typeset in Ines by M&S, Toronto
Printed in Canada

McClelland & Stewart,
a division of Penguin Random House Canada Limited,
a Penguin Random House Company
www.penguinrandomhouse.ca

2 3 4 5   27 26 25 24 23

Penguin
Random House
McCLELLAND & STEWART

For Charlie, who helped

Poetry's nothin' but a man feelin' what's there anyhow.

—RICHARD WAGAMESE

CONTENTS

THE
NATURAL
HUSTLE

THE NATURAL HUSTLE

Here's a thought experiment:
Imagine our fathers are together
glass blowing in hell.

Fine words for a soupe à
l'oignon spring afternoon
clarity of tablecloths and

consommé and clear blue
sky, hustling the clouds from
their front-row seats.

The natural hustle,
you told me, on the ferry
up, is being younger

than every other man in the pool
joint, involuntarily underestimated.
The great cathedrals to capital

woozed on by; crisply
glittering like cakes not meant
for eating, canted brazenly:

Not your fault if they
fall. That, you added, doesn't
make me a hustler. Didn't.

We watched a police boat, bobbing
for apples. The NYPD, they park out there
when the terror level is high

you said, in your tourguide voice.
If my dreams are any indication, the terror
level has always been high.

What the hell is that? I said, cupping
the skyline and you went: OMA is a kind of evil
architectural firm & their building

in Beijing is shaped like a giant M. Why
not? I thought. We should all be shaped like a giant
M. The wind altered its pitch an octave.

A little kid on the ferry was going
Is this true: even though I move away,
I'll still be a New Yorker in my heart.

You said: Sounds like someone's propaganda
worked; and the other kid went I don't care
about that, I only care about makin my movies

& then as we docked flung an arm about his friend's
shoulders, they went shouldering off together towards
Gracie Mansion, green plastic soccer fields, signs

reading GARAGE and just barely older boys
tossing bricks up the face of a three-storey from a
flatbed & the brick boys grinning, flash

of the sun's June teeth. I laughed
as always when watching men laugh
at work and remembered the night

before, that vision of smashed up silver
Lamborghini on Broadway at one a.m. like
a huge cicada, trauma-sprung wings

flailed high to the night, windscreen
atomized, and those pterodactyl-back doors
eyebrows, flung heavenward.

I scrawled you a postcard in the heavy hot
light: *Tell Anna I saw not one not two but three
French bulldogs being walked by this one*

*lady under the lavender expressway
by the stale fishmarket strand.* A car in the street
was playing Smokey Robinson;

Yes that's right I thought: take a good
long look. Sing it, Miracles. I squinted on into
the sun and thought of Russians and death

and that Spanish lemon painter you told me
about, of how he painted lemons yellow
as the jaundiced summer moon

yellow, and I thought of the stories
nations tell themselves, continual reframings
within which the machinations of

love death & personal politics grind on like
bagpipes or knives—*Gargle gargle* the
raucous tears of the dispossessed.

That's what I thought but you were saying
Alice Neel Warhol and Just look at Mantegna's dead
Jesus painting. *Gargle gargle*, I said

I have no idea who any of these people
are. Those officious skyscrapers, back on our trip up
river, the smart breeze and these signs

driving me crazy, like—Sign at ferrydocks:
GYROS PRETZELS CHECKIN KEBABS. This shit
just cracks me up, like how every time

I walk into a bar that punk
cover of What A Wonderful World is playing
& & whatever, gratis I grab a bowl of popcorn,

dig in, eavesdrop, check the messages raining
into my phone in blue and white droplets, e.g.: *I think you know
a lot more about history and atrocities than most people.*

Say you to me, sans irony. Fuck it, I just wanna be your
Joey Ramone. But these days there's always a Fleetwood Mac
song playing some goddam where, that's what

you call a Renaissance, I guess. And the leaves play
this particular pattern against the streetlamp against the galley
kitchen wall on Third Street at whatever time

of bluest dark each night and I personally think it's
perfect. I could watch this 'til forever, the icy noise
made by the light clinking. I have to tell you

this and everything. The river reeks of raw
sewage and general festivity. The scooter-eyed babies
bawling for a second chance, a smoke break.

Would you look at his ghastly body, I said, huffing the
stench of centuries dead rising off the Hudson. You're the one
who asked about foreshortening, you said.

I went to the store to get you beer and Glass
Tiger was gumming from the speakers like sticky
underpants. How has this grocery even heard

of Glass Tiger? I asked the checkout queen, who
deadpanned You want a bag for that? On the way out I walked
past this girl squealing at her ma How you gonna

tell me I cain't go to a Manhattan high school? Her
vowels as torqued as the wrung necks of rammed fledglings.
And her mother's concrete silence, a layer of gristle

upon which to go on choking, indefinitely. Uptown, we three
sit over mustard and frites and espresso and a sky beyond
reproach, and you remark on how abysmally bad your father

was at almost everything, which leads to the thought
experiment upon which no one wishes to embark. There are
so many ways to hustle clarity, obfuscate, cloud.

It's all a misdirection, like this jogging girl's t-shirt:
MY LEFT HOOK IS BETTER THAN YR BOYFRIEND'S.
Snake in the grass, today my silent hymn to the spring-

sick air goes Try me, try me. A man on Second
Avenue barks into his phone They haven't changed
since ancient times. They're still violent.

I don't disbelieve him, though I'm inclined
that way, in general, incredulous. Drifting in and
out of conversation steadily kir-sweetened,

I catch Esperanto: truly the language of misunderstood
seduction. I laugh into my coffeecup and a peppering
of midges as you tell Valerie how you were stuck

in a subway tunnel, locked in with a homeless dude
playing EasyJazz. Val cants her eyebrows like O the horror;
Yeah yeah, you say. On a boom box. For money.

If only I could make money like that, you say.
I whistle at the occasion of a crinkled white Fiori lowballing
by, like a messenger from that impossible country

where everyone I want to talk to is still alive. After this
we drive to Cold Spring, feel the cool supple fig
skin of plywood on our lolling backs, rest awhile; and

the bloodsucking hum of no-see-ums and the midsummer
light carrying itself cheekbone high into the evening and then
there is the Tarrytown moon, tarrying like a ritual tear

in a blue silk shirt, we ride south to Harlem where we eat
poisson grillé and drink pink wine and all night as ever Let's talk about
makin love go the speakers from everywhere.

SAVANNAH SUNSET

The sky was raked with colour
like the insides of a woman
fact of her flayed self
a bark in my throat
soft yelp of the drowning.

In the searing dusk a brown bird
took wing

angled into the night
acute

as she left us.

In the night she left us
angled into the wing of dusk
seared, a bird's

soft yelp drowning

the bright throat of her flayed
pink self, the woman inside
the sky raked with colour
that night she died

forever ~~caught,~~ a bird
in my throat inflamed.

A piece of the sky tore my hot
mouth, moaned.

Never once have I seen clouds
like that: her dancer's claws
stiletto red
the blood they drew.

RONCESVALLES

On Roncesvalles Avenue with the sun in the sky
right where last night's excesses left it, there is
plenty of unadulterated harmlessness on display,
like the worst thing everyone was ever told was Go
fly a kite! and not, The Wehrmacht have taken Warsaw.
Benches line the promenade with their cheery waft
of malt and urine and babysbreath, and balance the el
shaped legs of smoking men and the schoolkids' scooter
necks and the slat-pressed thighs of sunrumpled couples.

This pair making out are an amorphous mass,
their hands are everywhere. I imagine some old
guy coming along, out of the mists of the alley or a
film set in the 1950s, being like Cut that hair. A two-
headed monster annexing this patch of sidewalk,
they have the slink and wriggle of bangles or snakes.
They move like a thin-skinned animal swallowing
something hard. The stores are slowly closing, stale
bread o'clock. The crosswalk squeals. The couple
bellcurves. I just want them to be happy.

The airbrushed monkey puzzle mackerel sky looks
like a disease or an impressionist's hangover, except
for how shruggingly unapologetic its beauty.
How aberrant. Polish men stand on the steps
of the cathedral and use their cigarettes and hands
to play Pictionary in the five o'clock air. They can
also be found hiding behind a standup bass at the
local, along with other remnants from nearer wars.
The ballgame plays on TV, to general unconcern.

Outside on the wires teenaging the sky with their
badass black slits, it's like hawk hawk starling crow.
The go-ahead run goes ahead. The family portrait
is misconstrued. The insouciant waitress adjusts her tits.

On Roncesvalles Avenue, if you get close enough
to the water, you can still buy hard drugs or soft
women or a subway token for two dollars; and you
can fall asleep in the coyote wino clutch of the hope
green park or the stonewashed beach for free—or order
a fifteen dollar fried egg across the road where the
women paint their lips beetroot pink and turn their uneaten
brunches tiredly like tricks. You can buy a soft, bright
dress shaped like a man's workshirt or rent a truck for
the same pocketchange, drive it into a hydropole,
dieselstain slink into St. Joe's rehab and dry out.
If you get far enough from the water, everything's
so dry already it's drycleaned; except for the liquor
store cashiers, and the dollarstore stickyfingers, and the
rich, knackered, cash-creased mothers who are as desperate
to abuse the substance of themselves as the rest of us.

The rich mothers own dogs that can survive in the
water for days. The dogs can smell the lake a
kilometre away, and the meds sweating out through
the razed nuclear forest of their owners' lasered armpits,
and the piercing rapture of the toddlers at the sight
of a perishing dragonfly, a soccerball. The mothers
are sheltered from this sensory decadence by the
stifled shrieking of nerves in their hips and backs
that's risen up after thirty years like a sleeper cell
and now will never, ever shut up. The kids won't
shut up either, or the dogs, or the Facetime husbands,
wolfwhistling roofers, head offices on line one.
The only thing that will stay quiet until it goes away
is this street, this spring, just before sunset, just today.

That beautiful tree on King.
I remember it as though it was
yesterday, because it was. I said,
Would you look up at this tree?
Tree be like, I know the invite said
business casual, but I wanted
to get *decked*.
A spill of ochre ink,
like a couple of paint trucks
got smashed up,
decorating our Tuesday
with their demise.
If our blood were the colour
of old photographs,
and prone to fluttering
to earth,
we might bleed autumn, too.

Mostly it's just quiet here,
and the light wind,
and singing air.
You might dream that he wrote you a letter.
He did not write you a letter.
Look at that tree!
No one has written you
a letter.

The trees slurp up all the sunshine
and convert it into heartache.
The crispy angel frosting
moon still in the sky,

a snapped bulb,
phosphorescent, dilated,
fading on high.

UNTITLED 1969

Strakes of rain, and laths of cloud
and water, seamless joinery of grey.
The towers have been scraping
sky, they're plastered with it. The harbour
a private dick, undercover, the cloud-
spackled skyline. The lightless evening
in shards, shattered thermometer,
pulses of mercury on the windowpane.

Everything that is not grey in this picture
does not want to be seen: the monstrous wineskin
heart, trolling along like a man o' war, luminous
trails of unrebuttable regret braided among
the damp particles of the bay's pewter plate
calm. The water and sky meld like this year's
dead, consolidate. They are one thing, they
are everything. Grey rain on greyglass,
grey waves beyond, grey sky, grey clouds,
broken grey England one grey ocean away;
and the grey slog beyond *that*: tomorrow,
its brood of facsimiles, ashes and salt,
grey by dampening grey. And like breath

the phantom artist hovers, brash, mercurial,
exacting, flickering amid the raindrops—
those lucent little afflictions, pebbling
of stippled mouths, the tips of lickless
tongues untasted—and he's red all over,
fantastic, vermilion, dry.

ON THE SUBJECT OF INCREDULITY

I have no thoughts on this death.
Or, none that are relevant:
I have thoughts: I think: I don't
believe it. I believe this is a hoax,
suddenly I understand people who don't
believe in moon landings, or global
warming, or aphids, or empathy.
Why should they? Why should anyone
do anything she doesn't want to do,
like live, for example, survive?
Why should I survive the death
of another too-young woman,
another cracked mirror image,
headed for the crematorium floor,
a fine dust; why am I not so fine
as that, to be sprinkled, scattered,
parcelled out among friends and eaten
by the wind coming hard over the water
tonight, coming for the lightest of us
first, the incinerated grain of that darkness
you always saw in her, didn't you,
the fire, manifest.

I always meant to write a song for you
on Raglan Road. Then winter came, with its long
johns and bold cats and forty proof. I entertained
almost unidentifiable feelings in the basement's
blackout. It would have been better if I had left
some feelings unidentified, but that was never
my style, or rather lack of it: everybody knows
I've got no game. Anyhow, if I did, what would
we ever laugh about? I don't believe everyone
loves a winner, but I do believe we all crack
up sooner or later for a dirty joke, a groaner—
everyone loves a class clown, at least once,
at least briefly, because everyone loves a punchline
or a punching bag; everyone's punch-drunk, one time.
On Raglan Road, your hair started to go grey,
I want to say prematurely, except we weren't
so young. Mature is a polite word for it; but you
might say we skipped that part, headed straight
to rotten. I skulked around those mould-drowned
rooms in your rotten longjohns and felt a love
for you so perfect it was indistinguishable from
mourning. My love was so much more impeccable
than any human man, you may as well have died.
One imagines how it felt, in the crosshairs.

I missed you, daily, in plain sight, on Raglan
Road with the lost leaves of January shuddering
above your head in its permanent cowl of smoke,
and the unimpeachable soprano winter light sifting
through the wind's tin whistle, and the holes in your
socks, and in your shoes, and in that thing I called oh my
heart. The sky was a series of holes closely woven

as a sieve. I saw you straining through the winter's pores
into piebald tomorrow, halfdead with the life of it,
and your greys like the fuzz on stale bread or a
butterfly's wing, your woolen foureyed glare
all bergamot and black ice and brandy exhale,
and the smell of the numb, simmering earth and your
coat coated in cedar dust undusted and your safflower
skin, and I could see myself, as if from a treebranch
or a crow's nest or a copcar peeling past
on Raglan Road or near enough, at the edge of the
frame whistling "Raglan Road" out of key, fading.

SEPTEMBER GIRL'S GOT IT BAD

How do we quantify missing?
The leaves that have not yet turned.
The slap of autumn in the lung.
Requisite bite. Sharp sunslap smell.
The silk of it.

"The intertwining of the writer and the subject is the end
of the world. Like a nuclear reaction of despair."

When you say things like this, I wonder
if I am in love with you.

I listen to Oliver Sacks on the radio,
crackle.

Sing *September gurls do so much.*

I measure my missing in hot air
balloons. I can feel them pressing
up against the thin skin over my ribs,
aching for horizon.
I miss you so much: Next time you see me
my ribcage will be in a sling.

September girl's got it bad.

We will get coffee at a diner.
I will practically weep by which
I mean I will swear a lot and mumble
about the weather.

You will again say something
perfect and like the bloody leaves

pieces of me will go scarlet

and fall.

DONNA SUMMER

*"It's been a long but fast summer, if that makes any sense.
I think everyone's just eager to drop the puck."*
—Nazem Kadri

It's been a long but fast summer.
You considered emotions, rattling through
the paces half-assedly, zero to sixty, breathing
in a new and different way—the same way
a recalcitrant thirteen-year-old considers
showing up for class and having friends.

A long season of eviscerated woman-friends
and their damp, state-of-the-art infants, this summer,
tenderized, sewn up and sipped-from, considering
their scars, the pattern of milky light through
which a tiny skull glows, river-veined, that way
a fake ten shines under the blacklight, breathing

out its secrets. Another animal breathing
while asleep, a thing to behold. Friends
hardening and softening with age, way-
ward cells in revolt, wine. Every summer,
you entertain thoughts you've had before; through
a sweating glass, lacerated with heat, consider

whether there'll ever be enough July, consider
the menu, the news from Aleppo, the breathing
Chablis. You misapprehend, fail to think through
anything but your own righteous outrage, friends'
afflictions, your partisan posture. The summer
stiffs you with its snake charms, its coy way

of proffering summers lost, step right up, way
out past the shoreline of the viable. (Consider
a body, brassy as a Springsteen song with summer
brown, his so-long sweat-seared skin breathing
with its thousand mouths.) Fairest-weather friend,
this season, its smoke-and-mirrors seethrough,

its carnival of lousy odds, its ever ungentle We're through.
Summer's long but fast and it wants to go all the way,
staring at its watch. It perspires, it just wants to be friends,
it deals a deck of showstopper sunsets, considers
its chances, a leaf the shade of skinned knees. Breathing
hard for the finish, it uncorks heatwaves, summer-

squalls through the static-snapping sky. You consider
the options, the various ways of not breathing,
the absent friends. You play that song, all summer.

THE BOYS AT THE PIZZERIA

Drinking wine from a can from a glass. Wood
table, mittens. Moved in this way and in
that. The young pizza guys: doughty stand ins
looking like boys I might have loved. They could
have been, bouquet of zinfandel lips, good
hands, ranginess of youthlimb, easy grin;
the lush sweetness of it, getting things done, thin
skin at their collars blistering so you'd

want to soothe that itch with cool fingers, palms.
You'd have wanted that, once, and gotten—or
not; let the bombs go off all over your
body then snuffed the winedark flame of its song,
get lit again. Turned back toward the heat, youth,
rising like dough in the oven's hot mouth.

A man has to have his breakfast.
A man has to have his sad eyes.
A man needs the hair on his legs
and in his nose to filter out the
poison that tries to enter a man's
multitudinous many rooms even
before his breakfast has been
and served and gone; a man has
to have a filter, and a frame, for
that matter, a man is made of matter
and *alma* and body and soul he
cleaves to his mother who is with
him when he arrives to breakfast
on this slim and spinning platter
we call our tiny moment earth
we call unbearable. A man needs
to bear things, to bear off, to man
up, to telephone his mother, a man
needs to shore himself up against her
loss. A man has needs that bind him
like an infant's swaddling strips or an
electric chair. He has many rooms, a
man. He can be entered. A man
must be looked at by the faces of tall
buildings and women and the blood
dark moon, and called beautiful
like a spilled vein changing
colour in the light. A man's beauty
travels lightly, primed to pick up
and skip out on a dime, or to show
at your doorstep or breakfast in the
twinkling of a man's damp eye, really,
all you had to do was ask.

GOD AND THE PATH TRAIN

falling asleep on the PATH train
over some letters by Camus
re god and large feelings
I don't understand

one seat over
a teetering necklength away
a worried boy
        shifting in his cataract skin

my head and my book
go falling from my hands

I exit the PATH's tunnel into
a large square of light,
Hoboken, in which your idling wheels
at the curb. You want to dump sunflowers
all over Allen Ginsberg's grave—
I'm here for the ride

with the Hollies on the radio
deejay reliving some
golden elsewhere
I can hear his silvering breath
puffing under each harmony

baby, that's all, I'm like
—You know this guy?
—Sure I listen every week or something.

❂

Here's what we know about New Jersey:

The state's biggest industry was chemicals.

The state's biggest industry was poems about snow
that melts before it hits the ground.

The state's biggest industry was pages of a dirty book that stick together.

The state's biggest industry was pharmaceutical

glittering thing above the river falls

The state's biggest industry was death by

percocet or a door in the river.

❂

stand by the river which roils like a teen on the train
overlooked by the silk factory now empty windows
punched out susans and the split lip of water below,
—This place was known for its silk factories you say.
Shitty place to work. All of those worms.

I say what do you bet
you say what I say
nothing you say yes.

We get back in the car and drive.

❂

get out at the Jewish cemetery,
which is not short on Ginsbergs.

❂

In the car you told me about your friend
the Great Black American Poet.
You said your friend the Great
kept calling you My Friend the Great
Jewish American Poet—

I laughed so fucken hard

Spooky Tooth wailed for the wind,
turned over to Dave Clark
Five going Glad all over
like they were, all five of them
fingers on a glad hand
moving right along
into a receding hairline
of signs i.e. Home of the Whopper
as we drove:

Remember how in the old books
whopper meant *lie?*

If the lie is at home anywhere,
it's by the side of the highway
in New Jersey.

❂

We find him, of course
stone footnote to himself
a few rained-on pages
scattered like weather pulped petals

and then our sunflowers

and then a flush of starlings all at once
over the Ginsberg family sunbit stones
and all the stones playing
dead in that living field
(and the Stones playing Ruby
Tuesday out the car door)
and the groundless riverrush,
a flock of claw and tendon
that is only now and the now of it:
powerlines—Budweiser plant—
burnt barley on the air—
oh the graves
oh the stonebright clouds
        oh shit the car door
slamming like the sky's brief mirror.

And the road away.

Back on the highway, Ramones doing their
Cretin hop syncopations like a
bulimic mid-vomit like
this one song just *has* to leave my body,
a car cuts us off so close it's
practically driving backwards.

Sunflower dust on everything.

26

19th Nervous Breakdown plays us under the
General Pulaski Skyway, erected 1932 by state of NJ
then Stevie Wonder sings Fingertips
like they're his last remaining bodypart—
Willie Nile, well, ok..

Lackawanna goes a sign which could mean sandy creek or
where the stream forks or the stream that forks
or where the streams meet in Lenni Lenape
like every man's his own antonym
racing himself to the sea.

We are that soluble.

Actually they call that the Jersey Slide you say with ceremony
cutting across five lanes of traffic—that's its *name*.
I say You know what, Traffic's Paper Sun is the only
Traffic song ever to be played on the radio, fact.

Billboard: WHERE ARE YOU GOING
HEAVEN OR HELL?
Lackawanna I say, meaning *yes*.

And ok here's the story: General Casimir Pulaski
saved the life of noted jackass George Washington
at the Battle of Brandywine and General
Pulaski may have been a woman
they say, by which they mean inter
sex amidst the lives and deaths
of nations and his private
foot soldiers and limbs divisible
—Fruit from earth. Soul
from chest cavity—amid the carnival

carnage of the inbetween may have
spent long grey days in the saddle or
of rain in which he may
have been anyone, like you
me, or Shane MacGowan
on Christmas Eve.

(The idea is that one day you're dead
and once those who loved you
are also dead you are no one,
you are interpersonal
you are inter-air
inter-earth
interred,
entirely.
You are the scent
of eaten apples.
You are a mixture
of nothing
in mouldy
epaulettes
and your invisible shoulders
cannot hold
the flaxen braid
let alone
[withstand]
you.)

You say Yeah by the way that Broadway
play was great. Bullshit, I say.
Daryl Strawberry was great.
You say Okay, good then.

I can hear the ghosts of unemployed silk
worms every single time the deejay rustles.
I can hear the yellow graveyard still turning
like bad mayonnaise in the sun.

Every single thing on this highway in the state
of New Jersey and the world is moving.

Catch the water or your life as it falls.
Hop in.

More on Casimir Pulaski, who had a woman's
hipbones and they say delicate
face: *He gave his body to Savannah,*
gave his soul to God, goes one plaque.
My friend Savannah died young for nothing
and there is no god despite
the hipbones of her indelicate
body so let's have a fucking monument
to this one, sunsuckled afternoon
in which I sat in a sedan among sunflowers.

Let's cast the air in stone
lest we forget.

Let's all cling a while
longer
to letting it go.

The radio plays the scent of apples.
The radio plays the scent of cotton.
The radio smokes, and plays out its own exhale,
the radio plays the sound of beer going flat.
The radio casts a line of summer,
reels it in, a dirge. The radio plays the one
that got away, until it does.

—Oh this radio station you say
they love playing lesser Springsteens.
I Don't Wanna Go Home? Joe Grushecki?
Heavy rotation on this station you say.

Of all the revolutions
the American was stupidest.

●

You drop me at the station.

I sit here in a clean cool blue
plastic seat not caring less
about Camus who never
as it turns out even
once mentions the PATH train—
whether god is at the end
or Hoboken—I dunno
what people see
in the guy.
He's not a map.

The stations spin
past like golden oldies
asleep again
yellow dust in my hands

like ash—
or ash unexpectedly

platinum
in the fluorescence
that underground hail
of false, unwavering
light.

STUDY OF PROPORTIONS

You spent your life with a man,
first you were kids together,
then you had to mark things off
with an X: voting cards, moving boxes,
finally his name, like an honorific.
He became an X in a sketched ring,
your ex-man,
like Leonardo's beautiful nudes.

You could understand
why someone would want to
sketch naked men all day,
in between inventing things.

If you touch a beautiful man,
you have just invented the universe,
that alternate one, in which you laugh
and are kind to children and sway
on Ferris wheels and moral questions;

or you become another kind of inventor,
brilliant and windblown in the wilderness,
pigmenting the canvas with the fallout,
your great work, destroyer of worlds.

THE SNAPSHOT'S TALE: LONE WINDOW
ON A PORCH IN PASADENA

Let me stand here. Let me also look at nature a while . . .
Let me stand here. Let me delude myself that I see these things.
—C.P. Cavafy

In America in contemporary times,
probably spring, probably high winds
prevailing, possibly a rain of allergens, small
dogs, flowers, out on a porch in Pasadena
is a window observing an empty street
in the brick home in which it perches,
being photographed by a man without
whose presence today the home is also empty.

(In the suicidal mines of Inner Mongolia, the rare earth
is sapped to build a trap for transitory loveliness.
The smartphones grow incontestable eyes, and the
braying young grow double ranks of teeth; they grow
tumours instead of old, while you gain this reproduction.)

Art behaves at a fifth grade level and will never
get into college at this rate and time behaves
not at all, not if what you want to do is go back,
stretch those hands into the flatline
that precedes the heart's first sputter: keep it still.
Stretch a dead man back on his barstool, while you're at it—
freeze—stretch after dinner while the twilight spreads
its groundsheet and a crab nebula of stormcloud,
suspend that retinal blur and a scoop of satellites tenting
overhead, the atmosphere a shelter under fire.

The window, the wall, there's my tale, that's
all: the light bouncing off the Pacific, skidding
through a traffic of despair, splintering down from the
refracting hills, resting in the frame in two bright squares
like the ghosts of Buddy Holly's glasses; a vine
unflowered, a bottle full of blue air, and the man
stamped with all of this impermanence, reflected.

Today I'm a lone window on a porch in Pasadena.
Framing two sides of the same nonevent, hanging
out, out of context, clear. Spring, that mottled creeper,
lurking beyond me. Two-paned glare full of California:
buds, chiaroscuro, carbon, the shade rippling like a torn
Spanish flag, the light a chatter of Tongva transfusing
the atmosphere, the passing Priuses and indiscretions.

Step right up, see how I look like you, an echo of
hair and cotton, sodium, scar; backscatter of hopeless,
and heartschmerz and—oops, not too close.

Stand back a breath, or we'll become nothing
but the empty house that holds us.

IF ALL YOUR FRIENDS JUMPED OFF A CLIFF

Yes.

MAGIC HOUR, MANHATTAN, AUGUST

The city's histamine blush as dusk drips.
We seek a sportsbar 'cause you think it would
be nice if I could watch the Jays; all good
I say, as—the towers flush like stung lips—

I think walking next to you is heaven.
And I say, *Look at these buildings* [and you
look, nod] *in the witching light* [rose flange you
shuffle through]. It's as if they had been leavened:

surging tongues stained sweet nectarine, liver.
Every sportsbar is too loud. It's okay:
I'd rather watch instead the dying day;
my hometown sold me down the river,

long ago. The air we breathe in thins,
purpling.

It's enough the home team wins.

HOLLYHOCKS

The rain makes this knocking
sound on the windowsill
like some insistent gasman
at the door, full of beans.

The trees that no one knows
the names of due to laziness
ruffle and rustle at each other
like those women who complain
that other women never
like them. Everyone is too
lazy to identify the trees
as anything other than there,
to want to change anything
but the weather of other
women's lives. The sky
has gone deadpan, vacant
with cloud, sweating a
hot rain that quenches nothing.

Bang bang goes the tinpot
rain, up itself and loud,
evaporating where it hits.
The old Azorean ladies
wave a little polyester
and lace at each other from
porch to porch, fan themselves
with somnolent husbands'
hats, stoop in their sweat
like hollyhocks. Bang
bang! they shout, over the
rain and the wrought iron

railings, and the husbands
startle midsnore, *Sim sim*
as though someone had
asked them, drop back
into dreamless, peripheral
as pillars. The wind moans
and creaks like an orgasm
faked through the walls.
A siren wends its way
through chunks of distance
dodging the thousand failures
that didn't make the cut.
Like the last penny to your name,
the rain slips into the sewers,
rattling as it falls.
The wind subsides, purling
in its throat, and the leaves clink
glasses, lovely to meet you,
lovely, lovely.

And over and above all of this,
in the same tone as the funeral
priest going Above all this,
going Love one another,
I say, Fuck you rain. Fuck you.

RAISING THE BAR

The guy out back fingering his girlfriend.
Crackstrung sunbeaned woman teefing tips
right off the bar. The lacquered boys are back in town,
the girls leaving, pounding whiskey and high heels.
The patio tree contemplates scarlet cufflinks.
A man with rolled trouser cuffs sucks
at a cigarette like a cracked pen while the man
with no right arm taps the ghost of a heater
off his dried-out Bic.

Some bereft mother due north is screaming *Give us back
our children* at a streetlamp. Some onetime bombshell blonde
detonated and wracked is croaking *I can't find my boyfriend.
I can't find my phone. I can't find my beer.* What I
can't find is the year she turned twenty-two, or
I would give it back to her, like a firearm,
the Winchester life served her up instead, oiled, loaded,
cocked.

RECEPTION

je vois que je suffoque
—Réjean Ducharme

The tequila arrived
She combed his luxuriant beard with her fingers,
claws, a fist.

Four on the floor techno played on the astroturf.

The roots of the trees sat on the ruins like the calcified limbs
of a massive, extinct cephalopod.
Earlier, guests had consumed the body of Christ.

The light was green. This was artificial, the result of a plan.

Two little girls in white dresses danced in typical little flower
girl fashion, as though the speakers were an audience.
They would dance this way when very drunk, years later.

There was a wagonwheel of vines and flowers and candles
affixed to the roof, which was a tarp.
The treble was turned up all the way.

The couple appeared to applause and melted
again into the crowd's autotune.
Smoke wafting over the tables began to solidify.
Suddenly, it had girth.

The candles flickered so charmingly that people became convinced
that no time at all had passed. They began to use vocabulary
long abandoned. The wives looked at the other wives
as though they had never made newyears resolutions.

Shadows got dirty on the canopy above, grinding in ways the people below could only dream of, and did.

RAIN POEM

There is some
end-of-the-world
rain happening in
Toronto right now.

I can only imagine
that a fifteen year old
girl is standing in it
somewhere, getting
broken up with
by text message.

We may all fall
off the edge at the end
of the world,
in this rain
at this rate.

She's typing like,
Can't you even
say it
to my face?
and her face
is a half inch
underwater,
and rising.

Such is the downpour.

ODE FOR A BEAUTIFUL BRO

O! yer beautiful, bro
with your beautiful bro
hands blossoming into your
beautiful bro handshake,
knuckles first, o bro your
eyes are like limpets,
clinging to the remember
when bellylaughs of television
shows I will never see.
Beautiful bro, you have the
body of a renaissance
soldier, itching to pose o
bro you pretty scrap, trade
your girlfriend for a stuffed
divan and get real
about the business of lying
on things.

Sweet sulky bro,
turn your ballcap
round. Learn, beautiful
bro, the weight
of its shadow.

LITTLE GREEN

If you serve someone
whisky and beer
until his liver
ruptures what
do you do with his keys
on his
little green keychain
and how

did you find the driftwood
voice to tell the doctor DNR

and then
home,
a shower,
work—

which is the job of serving
beer and whisky
to living men.

PEACH FUZZ DECLAIMS & DRINKS CORONA

Three years!

Can you believe it?

I'm almost twenty-one, he said,
I slept at her mother's house

all the time.

I can't believe
she would
end that.

[his peony head beneath its
ballcap, wilting.]

Can I have another one please thanks.

She was like my wife.

That's what I remember: these real
dark nights. Ken or someone leaning
on the bar. The street like snuffed
candles, the shine on bruised and
swollen skin. The snow turning into
rain as Lee's hospital bracelets formed
a garland of reproof, sticky as the Jäger
splotched linoleum. Dull as the wood
showing through, the holes in the wood,
the roaches shaking from the shrill coats
of after dark women. Abortions, arson.
The inked faces foreshadowing the needle
scarred arms, even before the sleeves roll
back, like lips spitready, like eyes. Cops.
Men's faces hanging like stolen coats
from their hooks. The fratricidal opiates
of these midnight masses, cocaine burning
the fine hairs lining their nasal cavities
like singed insects, incinerating under
the gaze of glass and light. Rounds of
light pouring from the freezer at the rate
of real estate rising. The throats burning,
the books of matches. These real, dark
nights, everything burned and burned.
It was not as we thought then the light
that blinded us, but the ash.

POSTCARD FROM ICELAND

The weather is fine.
I cannot see for long
distances due to hills
but the distances in my head
lengthen. I have been thinking
about lava. How much cooled
rock does it take
to make a leg
to stand on?
These are the sorts of thoughts
I have here, on what you
people call vacation.

I have been thinking
of various wives
of my soul,
of my breakfast table,
of my dreams.
I have been trying to
arrange them, these ghosts
in an order that suggests
no order, that does not
insinuate rank. It has
been difficult.
I don't believe
in ranking things—
or ghosts, or women
that I, a man or a ghost
of one, have once loved,
which is to say continue to—
as love does not
simply stop

at nouns such as 'wife'
or 'forty' or 'yesterday.'

I have been thinking
of the Irish rain
moistening the skin
on the scalded milk
of my mother's voice,
this skin made of milk
and rain necessary for the
dropping tremolo
of a lullaby about a woman
who dies alone
and unmourned with hands
that reek of living fish.
I have been thinking
that my skin pulls
strangely over my bones
and that this causes
me to make simple
spelling errors
and poor decisions.
I have been wondering how
deeply into my head my eyes
could fall before the bones
in my strange exhausted
face would notice, sound
the alarm, realign,
resurrect. I am no longer
confident about the likelihood
of remedy.
(The bones might never notice,
I have decided.
My dawnstarched eyes could fall
through endless space forever,

like unhinged escape pods,
celestial garbage.)
The weather constrains,
handcuffs, a throat
inflamed.

My head is filled with
damp strips of cotton
that curdle and drip
like a fouled poultice.
The bombs in the heads
of others continue
to detonate while mine
just seethes and obscures,
dripping. There is the
reek of kerosene.

I ordered a cup of coffee today
then immediately threw it off a cliff,
right into the North Atlantic,
without tasting or paying for it.
I'm the king of this goddam
island, I screamed, foolishly,
as wolf fish and pollack
felt the pH shift in the water
and gnashed their snaggled
teeth at me.

I made myself a cup of coffee
today and stood over the kitchen
counter and the cup and the floor
barely holding up my feet
which cannot stand my body
from which my head hung
as it now hangs, by one

single, jealous thread
without which I would be
undone. I can barely
keep my head up.

The air is clean and
viscous and carbon
and I suck it back
like isinglass.
I can barely lift
my head for the air.
O god my head.

I'm not in Iceland.

I hate it here.

HERON

If only I were a
heron, my long legs in the
water, wingspan

pressed freshly as the morning,
and a mouth for stabbing things.

DEAR RANCHERS, WOLVES ARE KIND

Wolves are good. Wolves love cream cheese.
A wolf walked my daughter home once, *gratis*,
without ever trying to steal a kiss or jugular.
Wolves laugh, too, just like coyotes and landlords.

Wolves are a great species. They have been captured
on film. A wolf can suck on hard candy without
ruining her teeth. Wolves are pack animals, they
have self-restraint, they need no toothbrushes.

Wolves have hackles just like the ones that stipple
the backs of the women that you, Dear Ranchers,
touch without asking; the hackles rise and rise, a wave
of encomium, awkward gawking of the tiptoe crowd.

Wolves love summer for how much it resembles
winter, its elder sister. They love homemade popsicles,
how the juice that trellises down their silvering jowls
is made of real juice. Wolves have a powerful thirst.

I myself have known wolves. Tone-deaf, immune to
criticism, abandoned and admired by the pack, in
equal measure, wolves I have known have failed,
repeatedly, to keep their word. The lacerations linger.

Wolves I have known to be among the best of wolves.
I have known wolves with whom I would trust my
ranch, wrench my right arm from its den of tendon.
Some of my best friends are men who dress in wolfskin.

Dear Ranchers, wolves are kind as their kind can be.
Their kits eat the same snacks afterschool as yours do.
They acquire a taste for blood as you did, hot wolf milk
scalding their infant throats. Like men they have been

known to howl all night long—and to die,
right on schedule, before their time.

LOVE POEM WITH POTHOLES

1. Lonely people like to pour their full hearts
into q & a sessions.

2. You are my favourite season.

3. I loved it when you said It's not
that I care about averages. It's just that
everyone is much taller than I am
these days. Kids in middle schools.
Kids in spelling bees. Horses.

4. Your laugh like a grain of wheat.

5. The beautiful Ethiopian coffee lady
wears backless shirts.

6. A bank of melting snow, a lone crocus,
etc. Your wounded pawprints in the thaw.

7. Your mouth, the mouths of
other attractive people.

8. Pablo Picasso.

9. (Your smile when I said I don't care
if he was an asshole made me want
to live inside your mouth.)

10. Everything else was perfect
without me, and so are you.

BONEDOG

Coming home is terrible.
Whether the dogs lick your
face or not; whether you
have a wife or just a wife-
shaped loneliness waiting
for you, coming home
is terribly lonely so
that you will even think
of the oppressive barometric
pressure back
where you have just come
from with fondness
because everything is worse
once you're home.
You will think of the
vermin clinging to the
grass stalks, long hours
on the road, roadside
assistance and ice creams
and the peculiar shapes
of certain clouds
and silences
with longing
because you did not want
to return;
coming home is just
awful, and the homestyle
silences and clouds
contribute to nothing
but the general
malaise. The clouds,
such as they are,

are in fact suspect
and made from a different
material than those
you left behind.
You yourself are cut
from a different
cloudy cloth,
returned, remaindered,
ill-met by moonlight,
unhappy to be back,
slack in all the wrong
spots, seamy suit
of clothes, dishrag-
ratty, worn.

You return home
moonlanded, foreign,
the earth's gravitational
pull an effort now redoubled
dragging your shoelaces
loose and your shoulders,
etching deeper the
stanza of worry
on your forehead,
you return
home deepened,
a parched well,
linked to tomorrow
by a frail strand of
anyway:
you sigh
into the onslaught
of identical days, one
might as well
at a time.

Well, anyway,
you're back,
the sun goes up
and down like a
tired whore,
the weather immobile
as a broken limb
while you just keep
getting older.
Nothing moves
but the shifting tides
of salt in your body.
Your vision blears.
You carry your weather
with you, big
blue whale, a
skeletal darkness;
you've come back
with X-ray vision;
your eyes have become
a hunger.
You come home
with your mutant gifts
to a house of bone.

Everything you see now.
All of it. Bone.

SANDY KOUFAX'S CURVEBALL WRECKED HIS ARM AND IT WAS WORTH IT

It was perfect, and
by the end sheer agony
and it was worth it.

SOME LETTERS & ATTACHED PHOTOGRAPHS
(THE MOST BEAUTIFUL LEAF)

Have you ever seen Stieglitz's cloud photos?

You can see the movement in them,
the fluffy burlap sack of several kittens
fighting to get out.

↳

Oh, love, send me November, a
picture of the most beautiful leaf,
doused in Man Ray's tears.

↳

I never heard of this fish.

↳

Did you know the Russian
equivalent of a black sheep
is a white crow?

↳

The *ballan wrasse*.
It doesn't even sound
like a fish.

Thick bible lips & the young
like grassy
gemstones.

꒷

After I told him Tall Drink
O' Water died, OD or whatever,
he said Her death does not
define the neighbourhood.

And yet, nonetheless, the
neighbourhood
is dying.

꒷

The lung you took for granted
flatlined
at the wreckage
of the former safe injection site.

꒷

My best friend writes me
regarding his pre-
mature ageing and
endless toil.

Some chimps bust free
of the zoo in Belfast.

Go chimps go! we cheer,
stupid with jealousy.

꒷

The dark California heat
and light of your camera.

Now I depend upon your camera
all is lost.

꙳

The moon the moon the moon the moon!

꙳

This lady in Detroit gave me a side
of fried mushrooms
no charge.
Who cares if they didn't taste
like much? Honey
you've *got* to try
'em, she said.
I loved her.

Even now, as I write this,
I love her still,
bag of greasy chips &
the pulmonary crack
of Michigan night.

It was so cold the skin
on the thighs of the good
time girls was stuttering
as they smoked.

꙳

Italian doctors invented Syndrome K.

What have you invented?

*

All the air looks great
from this side of the water

but my friends out there tell me
it is
so terribly cold.

*

Rhys sends a photo of the north
tip of Miquelon
in the fog.

Everyone sends a photo,
the antidote.

Don't blow your brains out yet,
for there is mercy in this world.

*

«Il n'y a point de belles prisons, ni de laides amours.»

Oh, really?

*

You send me a picture of a streetlamp,
for scale.

What is that, a baobab?
A mission fig. Well, well.
I know nothing about California.

Well, look at that tree.

One can hardly breathe, despite the light.
One can hardly
anything.

⠀⠀⠀✒

I know you're busy but guess
what I just discovered?

There's a French verb for
to take on the colours
of the rainbow.

⠀⠀⠀✒

Here is the base of a fig tree
like snakes.

Here are some photos of the sky
over Port aux Basques.

⠀⠀⠀✒

You're lying in your own
beanbag mood, he whirs, on the
tail of a shimmering ellipsis. The
words appear in ballooning blue
bubbles against a snow-white
field: a perfect sky's negative.
My beautiful friend is all *post-*
radiation and a glass of late night
wine and *bowl of berries*
watching television and has been

texting me things like, *Sitting in sauna.*
Pen marks on my body.

My beautiful friend
is a bowl of berries
late at night.

Inking his great love
on the world's glass flanks
in stained relief.

࿔

I suppose it's what happens
when a largescale event is going on outside
you; there are also these tiny
momentous events within

and

—warm earth
hitting cool air in a gibbous swell
of steam, frog's expired
backstroke, hollow
puff of
gut

a hot spark on slick water—

lopsided,
they match.

Perhaps this is the poetry of a world
in crisis, Alec says.
Yes, yes, perfect.

When has the world ever
not been in crisis?

I too think the world might be
a love poem.

Man at bar asks for two shots
and my hair down.

(I never said a good one.)

You send me a picture of a blue
raven in a diamond of chainlink.

The cameo

of coal in my throat.

You write me, *And a brief
ballet.*

You write me, *That line was written in wet
cement on the sidewalk on my street.*

I lie in wet cement at the end of the street
& wait for nobody to notice.

A brief ballet of cocaine and babysbreath
drifts down from the condo balconies.

❧

("maybe a book is a long poem
the way a panorama is
a long photograph
or one of those really wide shots with incredible resolution that you
   can
zoom into and see
tiny people with great clarity
doing their tiny things.")

❧

[The condos lean on an anorexic scapula
of sky, dry heaving.]

[They shed their invisible dander.]

I rise. The cement
does not cling.

❧

Tell me your dreams

but only if I'm

in them.

A checklist:

· One of the things I will read you
  about the siege
  of Dien Bien Phu involves a nurse
  and a bottle of champagne.

· Meatballs and regret, television
  & rockets.

· I adjust my clockradio back
  one hour.

· This could be the winter
  of the evening grosbeaks.

Then you went to church in a dream
with your grade one crush.

You opened your heart to her;
and she was crestfallen.

All they did all day was play
Another One Bites the Dust

at that stupid bodega all through
the falling winter of 1980.

Meanwhile, downtown,
John Lennon was dying.

꙳

Like a pinecone, pocket this.
A reminder of the season
I felt everything for you.

꙳

A man at the bar says, I miss
your dry humour and your loveliness.

My aunt pulls out an old photo
goes, We look like kids.

꙳

Poetry is that slowsong.
Every wedding needs one.

꙳

(And every bride an elegy,
veiled.)

꙳

What I think riding the clacketyclack subway
past another flat-tire spew of faces:

I wish I'd fallen for another city.

I think of Eric and how much he loved the Allman Brothers—
like he loved each brother individually.

I think of Dennis and his barbershop quartets.

The faces turn

like leaves.

꙳

This man at bar talks about
the guys he did time with:
"He was gay, but boy could he
fight. Could he ever."

His cool beer bottle
sweats hot tears

for him.

꙳

I can't even be lonely
in a conventionally acceptable fashion,
like this bitch on the radio.

꙳

I ride the vomit comet amid the winter snow.

Disgorge at Greenwood Yard in the
blackest gut of night.

Didn't capture the glittering nor the magic nor the
stateliness of the trees but on the plus
side the phone & its camera.

I hope I didn't wake you
with this
surplus
of beauty

I say, spinning in the snowglobe,
waking the dead flakes
into flurries
from their banks.

༄

God that moon
is all I ever say.

But god that moon.

II

The flakes of night.
Oil of a fingertip.

Snow that is mostly
a tree.

Snow that is mostly

several trees.

—a bird
yesterday look you can see the blood
upon its beak.

Noble and beakly in
death.

Wingly and clawly.

I save you this photograph on my tongue.

BELUGAS

"The problems are huge. But who cares?"
"Whales are also huge."

You say you are spinning your wheels,
that you can't see the beauty in it, there's none.
You wonder what Jack Gilbert, a dead man
from California, might have to say about it.
I say Perhaps there is beauty in it, though.
You are unconvinced; or, framed otherwise
I am unconvincing. I need a different
frame, you say, so I can see the beauty
in this. *This doesn't feel like beauty.*
He might ask you what it does feel like.
(A dead man from the coast who was an expert
on—what else?—the beauty of certain
thigh-brief moments: a woman's startled
skin in a bark of sunlight, the pucker
of seawater drying, and the sulphurous fizzle
of the soul's involuntary blackout, Jack Gilbert,
you say, flunked out of school, just like me—
and *I* would ask you, What does it feel like?)

Maybe beauty's not supposed to feel
like beauty. Maybe it's supposed to
feel like wheels spinning off all the hairs
on your body until your body is just sore
bald skin and you can feel everything,
including the beauty. Maybe your wheels
aren't spinning; maybe you don't have
wheels—maybe you have *whales*

and they're spinning because they like it,
rolling over and over and over in the
ice-spleened Atlantic, spinning like
white winestems in the palms of half-
bagged mothers, spinning like kitestring
spools in the hands of children
caught out in the lie of their own
sufficiency, flayed for fun
by the ample, ripcord wind—

you have whales: pods, gams, flocks of them
happy golucks, bullish, buoyant, bright
dervish savants afloat with the certainty
that if yr blubber's thick enough the day
is always fine, all that hypothermic
ocean wash feels good,

a cool towel on a boxer's neck,
right over the spot, if you could
see it, where his trainer kissed him,
deeply, just before the bell.

LIST

Things I could give you:

A crab at the bottom of a boat
a headstand
nine hail Marys &
eight plaster Jesuses
a toast
a cooking pot
a pearl of penguin bone on
a beach
the apology on the inside of
my mouth
a soil sample from Prince
Edward County
a lateslip, an eyelash,
a high note, a ribbon
of tightrope.
A noon-streaked crown of kelp
or a handful
of sunlight.
A sabbatical.

A pair of sneakers & a
summerdress
on your floor
at last.

FUEL ECONOMY

He was in love with her when they crossed the border.

The words from the church drifted over: poverty;
dream. It was warm in the sun.

On Tuesday they made yogurt. The morning
smelled absurd, it had the texture of a paper hat,
a joke in a Christmas cracker, it was crème de menthe
and bear paws, a sticky summer barstool.
It pooled at his feet, around her head like blood.

When they crossed the border, he was in love with her:
he loved watching her drive, controlling the radio,
wagging the cigarette in her teeth like a conductor's
baton. He loved watching her back into a space
in the bar's parking lot, order one of everything
for closing time, suck his dick in the men's room.

It is safe to say he was in love with her before
they crossed, and after, as this feeling dwindled,
still, it ran on fumes a hell of a long time.
That's what you call fuel economy.

TEMAGAMI SUNSET, FAR FROM HOME

I closed my eyes and saw Temagami
as though it had been waiting for me, slow
as its sunsets, patient as the dark sea
stare of its rubberlipped moose; and the low
hum of nightfall, bassline to the solo
of a billion high virtuosic stars.
How does this hope thrum in you—oh,
and why? It glories in its thousand scars;
sudden beauty in the blood like cesium,
its unholy surfacings: I did not
know these waters lived in me, dark lesion
of June lake, ache of chances hope forgot.
The dead stars, howls of light resurrected.
Dead love fights for breath when least expected.

There was beauty in America and I found it.

Everything was free: the deer, the libraries, lunch.
It was a hitched ride with the fire chief, this free

and fine America, the sailor who gave me a ticket
for a Cessna flight up the coast at dawn

the rocks brimming out of the salt blue
like knuckles ruddy with victory—

and the Cessna bounced with every invisible
pothole, every clump of air we hit and the man

next to me read a book and below us
there were islands and mist spidering

like lifelines along the water, best suit blue.

This America a tiller in the hand,
bearing away.

There were orchards, bears, rivers
of morning and dusk and rain

and pickups stopping to offer
a lift as far as the fork in the road—

and there the tamarind-breasted
warbler would peck at the night's harvest

of skittled junebugs, then the bright rain
and the dark black beauty of the woods,

I found beauty in America

where the daily boxscores told the tale
of someone winning, and no one got shot

under the large American moon
that sang itself white in the April nights

as though it were made of light,
as though all lies were always

this pretty.

MY HYPOTHERMIC MOURNER

I think you're looking for the wrong
thing, a lifering of solid
plutonium.

The cant of T-squared
answers in a world of
animal fluidity

joie de vivre of
gulping spore in
blackest forest;

a liquid lung.

Every rotten body
is a blossom.

The heart recracked
an efflorescence.

Viruses and dirges
triumph, the fluid air
a conduit, riverine.

Its mortal lightness.

That you must move through like a
fox or a silk scarf
[scarlet hint at the frame's
edge, vanishing]

in which you must burn and cool
and metamorphose
steam off the lake
of your longlimbed youth.

Nobody made
little green apples

but oh

they taste

so heavenly.

WHILE WE STILL HAVE BEES

If I lived in America, I would bring you honey
while we still have bees to make it for us.
I would make you a new America entirely from
honeycomb, long nights of sleep, lemons to scald
the throat sore from the hemorrhaging of headlines.
The world-wracked throat craves sweetness as
in their chains of rhythm old songs ache towards resolve.

Sometimes I'm Happy is a song
by Doris Day who sings to you throughout your
cold sweat in the lonely American fever that trails
you all the way up the choking ocean's coast.
(Take pills to sleep rest yourself
rest is an underplayed B-side.)

From within their coils of discord the people ply
themselves with cheap resolution.
The old songs dissolve in your salt body
like the pills, occasioning new and wondrous tides.

There is no nightmare like that of waking.

Doris sings, *My disposition depends on you* and you wake
up freezing on a dwindling Arctic floe of soaked sheets.

I look more like hell than normal, you say.

I cannot tell, from here, if hell is normal
or if hell is worse.

A CHERRY-RED MG ROADSTER ON PALMERSTON SQ, JULY, 2020

In the weeks after Savannah died,
I would see things
in their new, unholy
light, stripped, as you do—

here's one, Palmerston Square
in the magic excrescence
the snow globe of glow that remains
of a sunless July evening,
I take the alley shortcut,
its mercenary efficiency
carving through the flanks of prim
brick, northwest toward Bathurst.

All the old nameless alleyways
have signposts now
like department stores.
As with affairs, being named
they end soon after.

In the weeks after someone dies,
you think about them all the time
in the act of *not* thinking about them:
I'm not going to think about it, I think,
sharply intaking the filigree light, a scalpel—
it isn't true, I think, clocking the
cherry-red MG, casually resplendent, in the drive—
I'm not thinking about her—
young girl practising flute in the window—
her *then*-ness or her *not*-ness,

jangle of hoops, tattoos and dotted cotton,
a shed snakeskin
her summer dress unmoored.

The young girl mouths her flute,
the notes wet the evening air.

Down the street, the knife-sharpener's bell
warbles, nearing.

VARIATION ON AN ELEGY

Another still in
another album, or an
anywhere of dirt.

Your throatless a cappella,
an electric song unplugged.

DOOR PRIZE

There is a slang to all jobs, like there is a
romance in each office block—
when you're a courier on the road
hard or slackass through the weather's
doggerel, and you get slammed, passenger-
sided, Henry Forded in the ribs or hips or
unlucky you, bloody milktooth mouth
(That a ketchup sandwich, or are you
just happy to see me?) they call it the
Door Prize. Comes out of nowhere,
much like everything else.

He used to slide into your Sundays that way,
a flung T-bone, perpendicular skid into disaster,
ricochet your day of rest from macaroni to straight
bourbon, flick of the wrist. Hauling on his
cigarettes like transatlantic flights. Like each smoke
was a mainsheet he was fighting, against the gale.

I didn't slide into your goddam
Sunday he'd say, you rammed into mine.
I was just minding my own business he'd
say. You'd go, The body is neither a prison nor
a cage nor even a metaphor for those things—
or anything other than what it is: a green tree
in a spring garden. Keep it down, he'd say.

Bruise-driven and road-wracked you tried
to bargain your body away, first for the untendered
shade of the solstice noon, then the drowned rat
Atlantic, finally the maw and paw-shaped chip
in his shoulder. The calluses started flaking

off your fingertips. That wager you made
of your own flesh. The failed rhyme of gristle on steel.

You said, I need to become an Olympic record broken
or a drag king's spirit gum or the angriest man in the room,
the evacuation of Dunkirk, anything itching the brink
of something else, anything but a tree or a sidewalk or a cage.
A bear—with its paws and fat and fierce and limblength
stride and winterlong, and that winter heart
of a bear which is larger than a hospital, a closefisted
cross or the moons of Jupiter even, or falling in love.

He'd say that love is not a closefisted
cross and you'd say, Is that the mouth you
cross your mother with? Simmer down, he'd say.
I am not a beautiful woman on your couch,
you would remind him, or an old man in a dive bar
on Bloor Street, I am not the girl who will
blow you in the alley for five dollars—not even
a shortstop, or a brontosaurus, or Willie
Mays! Simmer down, he'd say. I never said you
were Willie Mays. The park through his window
one frozen syllable, speechless with new snow.

It was not yet spring. The list of things we weren't
is longer than a hot shower, a cricket match,
that awkward eulogy pause: He—I—we—
(Tissue.) Excuse me. I'm sorry. Forgive me.

You can choose to ask forgiveness, but you might
not get it, like every damn Sunday of your life
you can bet that dark horse'll show and still die
poor. If you deny being a bear with a bear's irascible
paws and heart and appetites, you might
get booked as a beautiful woman, give

the wrong impression. The correct words are Yes,
officer. No, officer, I've never done this before.
I swear it came out of nowhere.
There won't be a next time, I swear.

DUBLIN HARBOUR TALE

If being told is what you like
I'm your man, until I tire of
telling at which point I will be
a tired woman, tilled, untold;

I'm your man, until I tire of
caterwauling at the tight sky,
a tired woman, tilled, untold,
too shipwrecked to tell anything.

Caterwauling at the tight sky,
voice gone throaty with lost plot,
too shipwrecked to tell anything,
I head for the port where nobody talks,

voice gone. Throaty with lost plot,
coursing the shade of a stevedore,
I head for the port, where nobody talks:
just yelling, yelped orders, and silence

coursing. The shade of a stevedore's
cracked mitt above his pterodactyl eyes,
just yelling yelped orders. And silence,
the muted tide's catstongue licks,

cracked mitts. Above, a pterodactyl-eyed
gull chokes on a sixpack's plastic silhouette
while the muted tide catstongue licks
the concrete toes of the refinery. A yahoo

gull-chokes down a sixpack. Plastic silhouette
towheaded boy waits for his bus by
the concrete toes of the refinery, *Yahoo!*
office block. Two tugboats gurk past,

tow, head off the boy awaiting his bus. By
and by, it will come, his mother will look up:
office blocks, two tugboats, gurking past
the boy's eyes reflecting concrete swaths of lawn.

Boy, it will come. His mother will look up,
and bus, barrage of seaweed stench, receding sea,
the boy's eyes, reflecting concrete, swaths of lawn
will grey; the boy will grey, the port, the sky

and bus. Barrage of seaweed stench receding, sea-
black, the dusk will tide in, high water
will grey the boy. Will grey the port, the sky
quiet, empty as a grave, unsewn as

black dusk. The tide in high water
telling at which point I will go
quiet, empty as a grave unsewn. As
if being told is what you like.

TATTOO

I would like to print myself on your
forearm, and then shower myself off
and become something new underneath
your shoulderblade and then change my

shirt and turn into a word that sits on your
skin for the forever that is the length of one
hour in the morning, the sixty minute stretch
between Ah that's early and You're late I'm late
I said you would be, my stain would swim in
formation above your muscle tissue and below
the epidermis for long enough to let the
rat-a-tat-tat of light hail on the bedroom window
and in my throat which catches like a Gatling
when your hands run like ink from your arms
and pulse, anemones, seeping where they may.

Mostly I just want to sit around and be like
God you're beautiful. Or I could slouch about
writing titles for sad country songs.
I want to affix such viewpoints to the running
rigging, hoist them high enough to see
from your roof. Heave away.
I want a chemtrail of God you're beautiful
to fly over your house today.

Meanwhile, broken hearts abound in the city's downtown
broken heart district. I am strongly considering
being the next disaster. Things need to be prevented
from rotting, somehow: we send for bags of ice,
congeal in drywalled eyries, fan our lovers
with mothwing hands and good intentions.

Our good intentions soil and singe
the skin on our fingers, set fires
where they are not wanted—
until we are not wanted, with them.

AUTUMNSONG

These are the days of deepening, the cool
trees giving up a blush of ghosts, vein-dark,
winds westing in from the coast, hungering, stark
with the marrow of honeysucked hours, pools
of freshwater sky bruised as pupils, jewel-
sleek as morning rain rattles like a toast
on sun-slaked eaves; arbutus at their posts
weeping flank the blocks, greenly keening fools
for September, as Mary says she loves
the deepblue year, this digging to the bone
of days, the bite and ravening, whetstone
air honing breath to blades, fingerless gloves
of mist clawing the slopes round Horseshoe Bay.
Summer's spine snaps: the chilling light at play.

SHE AWOKE TO THE RAIN AND FALLING SHEETS
OF FRUIT AND LIGHT

At night in the park the lightning strikes never,
because it's sheet lightning, bedsheet blanketing
the sky over the grounds where people have died and
failed to die and been memorialized and yearned at
and broken up with armslength long in a tree and forgotten.
All these things have happened in the park, and now the
lightning above it, and the rain that moves sideways
like a crab or two adults falling in love.

The storm is not frightening anyone and the farmers
need the rain, the crops need it, and the bank accounts.
Most days, the park is full of women feeling things and observing
their own legs under harassed fringes of cutoff cotton.
They point their painted toenails, and the gloss catches
the light the way the sky does, wholly.

Everyone is from just up the road or just down the road
and so we meet in the park by uncoincidental chance to
catch up on bones broken and debts due or what's for lunch,
who's the favorite, when we'll see you. Soon, soon. We chit
and chat as is expected of us and look up and say, "Rain tonight."

My friend sleeps in the grave of our banter in which he is
always awake. We just quote him as if he were alive,
we speak quickly, and move on. I move on the way a brigantine
that has run aground rocks and ruts in the silt at the bottom
of the channel: I heel, I tender. I take sides. I do not move on.

The sky is fluorescent, the raspberries on my toes
and mouth mashed, the rain is whipping the shingles
like they're a batting cage, like they did something

wrong, and the wind hoovers and yelps, strobe-violet
violent as a berry black bruise, each uppercut leaf wet
as a Norway spruce, or moss, or a woman. The sectional
leather couches in the condos are unmoved and the permanent
hair of the wives and the oil-on-canvas highway is a video
game still like the gallery-glazed wars of yesteryear, while tonight
in the halfcut park the sky is not split apart; merely pulsing

with replacement slides of another sky and another,
dis-coloured, soused sapped aubergine, high-lit, fallen
fruit dark and fierce as dogteeth and oh that rain
that rain

"Gardening is an occupation for an old man,"
he tells me. The old roses have fallen
as has the old government. Graffiti
compares the powerful to holes
in women or trees.

Because the mayor is a decent guy
the biscuits are shaped like roses
and the young men are shaped
like ads for cologne.

There is a pink rose
tied around my neck, a reminder
of the impossibility
of ever leaving.

In December everything was suddenly made
of everything else: the Audi's steering
column a flexing bicep filled with pure
Russian vodka. My pepperspray heart
going off, an explosion of capillary
roses, cologne-doused.

There was a man with olive groves for hands.
His hands were well known.

Death was a kite we flew, far above.
(We could feel it, tugging.)

The new government is now falling also.
There are no roses with which to compare it.

Like the city walls, the women do not care
who marks them. This much is unchanged.
The women open up under the assault's
attentions, and become a meaning.

Graffiti blossoms nightly and the walls and
women go on bleeding, petal-red.

The old men no longer concern themselves
with fruit trees
and in defiance the fruit trees
are vanishing.

HARBOUR

It is possible
to never get out,
to live this way your
whole life. Slivers of sunrise
hemorrhage, scatter
themselves askance
throughout the lean,
heatdark day.
It is possible to do
almost anything.

Down in the water,
the fish stay cool.
Above them,
your toes hang
like clouds.

TELEPHONE LINEMAN, 1964

My friend and I went and walked
on this really busy road
to the candy store which was dangerous
and far and somebody told
on us, and we ran hiding
from our parents,
and I hid in the garage.
    And Billy,
my friend, had a very tough father
and he was gonna get whipped,
but when my father found me,
he just kind of took me
aside and said, Do you understand why
it's really dangerous for you to do that
at this point in your life,
why it's really dangerous
for a five year old to walk a mile
along the highway to the candy store?
And I felt really pleased
at that point
that he was my father.

I had this dream when I was a kid
I fell out of a car on Hicksville Road,
and there was all this traffic, and I was trying
to get to the other side
but I couldn't walk
I was just kind of dragging
myself and I had to get out
the way of this car and I just—leapt—
and I smashed my head
against the wall

where the bed was,
and woke myself up.

Funny how you can look back
at life or a dream you remembered, you can
look and look, but nothing changes.
Like some old film, reanimated
stays trapped within the frame.
Still by still, the ghosts remain
opaque. They do not know
they will become a grandfather,
move to California, stop
breathing. They stand there
in the garage, tenderly.
Uncrowded by details like
the future, the play of light
and dark, a few metal hooks
biting into splintered wood, the smell
of gasoline: the scene is spare
of everything
but fear, and tenderness.
I see him looking down
at this petrified child
like a wild animal, I can see
the whites of my eyes.
And being so gentle.

Things were different at Billy's place.
There was something about Billy,
the toughluck tendril of his life,
shooting off. And now he's dead.
Did I tell you that? That people
from my gradeschool could be
dead amazes me.
They were children. We held hands

especially with Paula, got
suckerpunched, kicked, dreamed
in crayon, sat, waited in line
endlessly it seemed though
the lines led nowhere
and then recess. Yes,
I got beaten up a lot,
but not at home. Billy,
I don't know how he died,
hadn't known him since
we were eleven and he turned
into an asshole and I moved.
Perhaps he was beaten into it.
I couldn't say.

His father was a giant
and a phone company lineman.
He was tough with his boys
and very careful with
and protective of me.
I felt like he treated me like a girl,
for which I was grateful
and also ashamed.
I think he knew
that I was not like his sons,
and that they picked on me.
I don't know how he died, either,
or how Billy felt about it.

He did switch to Bill, eventually
when we were older and he was
an asshole I never really knew.

Dear Yesterday,

Out here the gunsel dark descends,
mercenary, unattached, packing; staggers,
flaps its greatcoat, leers. The palms
looming like unilateral measures.
Trees here are made of asparagus, it's true:
here, let me paint you one,
crowned with a memory of light
that runs like blood off the Volga.

(Naturally, all sorrows melt away
into the quality of the light bleeding
through Shishkin's beard) (but still I
wake up full of longing.)
Can't shake it.

The tinsel sunset strings, the clouds
funnel and the people drive and drive
until they pull over,
wait for the torrent to starve itself
into the deathmask of a rainbow.
The light a wound annotated
by various birds.

Yes, I woke up this morning in America
filled with longing. It is a trap.
(We are trapped, I think.)
(I'll speak for myself.)
I am trapped.

(Like the thousand brunches acclaimed
weekly in lavish online obituaries,
dreams can be too pretty.
Look—[a woman licking honeyhued sleep
from the corner of her ex-husband's eye]!
Even mine.)

I never want to go to the Rose Parade.

Today I saw a tiny dog dangling from a thin
woman's wrist while she swayed like a maquette
of a condominium doomed to fall. The dog
wore a little suit and dripped from the woman's
cephalic vein at the angle of a charm on a bracelet
or shit fleeing the sphincter of a minuscule dog
beneath a Californian palm, the embroidery on
his suit itself stitched by tiny mice, now dead.

All the trees here as I said are coiffed
like the heads of women on death row
or *Vogue* magazine and appear later
in salads made famous by the internet.

It seems here at last the light too
is dying of exposure.

It's not Siberia, no—but it's something.

As ever,

Pacific Standard Time

DARK-EYED JUNCO

I love how you turn your eye on me and don't see
me, I love how you look through me with a love
you can't feel, the way I feel about a hydroelectric
dam I guess: monumental, misplaced, alive.

The moon's electric blade curves in me like a bad
check, the dry plains of April lawn solar panels
cracking beneath the weight—mine and the work
that is transposing light. Take a load for free.

My favourite songs are dry leaves gone green.

My favourite part of photosynthesis is the guitar
solo. My favourite thing about this dark-eyed
junco on the treebranch out my window is its
improbable, stoppable heart, like mine—how we're
both here, unlikely story, not yet gone, not built to last.

STEELTOWN RAIN

Lines five and six, second stanza.
—Leonard Cohen "The Old Revolution"
   (Which I cannot afford to purchase from Sony)

It's none of my business.
Nothing is.

Just another easteregg
playoff season rain.
      This rain
in solidarity
with the absent
orange groves of
Jaffa
with the teenaged ghosts
of Attawapiskat
the Ticats
the holy martyrs of north
Scarborough
with the FAS jaws
twitching down the
street and the Adidas
stripes shifting dope from
heel to wakeful heel;

for the nightshift's
shattered override
for the beat cops in
the coffeeline

rain of garbage days of pizza
box and Budweiser,
the abortive aspiration
of old men's belts

and the yearly masochistic
parade & its cruciform grief—

here's to life, and the
drenched gutters rising
in counterpoint
to the people
who settle in its
troughs like sediment;
who are played
like pipes or plump
pigeons, heading
for the fall.

Here's to the
monster truck prams and
the swinging dicks & the
playoff fever and the stupid
pink headbands of the infants
w/ their tumorous bows;
and the kids in hoods
with ears and the
grownups in hoods
w/ ears and the
kids who died because
their shirts had hoods
and to the hoods themselves
because no one deserves
to die, no one deserves
anything—& to the boys
in the bay,
mouths gummed
up with flabby bleached
bread, prison butter

and jam
b/c no one

deserves anything
but you get it anyway,
don't you, right in
the teeth,
right in the cakehole,
you get what you get.

꿀

Danny's ma skipped
out when he was just a
walking baby boy,
forged too many
cheques on his dad's
account, treated other
men with the cash.
You know what I'm saying?
Stole the dough and showed
those guys a nice time.
You know the drill.
When his dad went one
day to the bank and they
asked about where's all that
money gone, and he stumped his
hard finger down and said
That ain't my signature
and went home, where he
found her, no words required,
after which said I won't call
no cops and I ain't gonna
charge you and I ain't taking

back that scratch but now you
leave, you leave now get
out the fuck from this house and
when he said that also
he said And the boys
stay. And she left.

And Danny says fifty
some years on sucking
back a cold Molson
Canadian lager Yeah
my mother was a bitch.
But my dad was a hard
Irish bastard anyway he
beat on her and on me, too:
you get what you get.

So you're driving in this
pissing up a tree rain and this
footless old sock of a
man's begging & shuffling at
Parkside and Bloor just as the rain
starts to really pour and pummel
windshields and newsprint shelters
and the big, white
SUV up ahead's a humming
tension gushing hot clammyass
rain as the man's making pleading
please please faces and the light will
never change and the great white beast
purrs its robot window down,
hands over a twenty.

And the twenty's torque &
shine in the driving
hotknife
rain.

And the guy runs
for his girl under
the bridge like fuck,
let's go score.

And it goes on, it
went on raining all along
Lake Shore like your life
was one big

car

wash

rainrainrainrainrain
like it's rain's
graduation day
and this is its big
sendoff like pomp
& circumstance of
rain like Motown
man ain't supposed to
cry rain
like a girl is dancing
in it that mud-ribboned
citypark lawn of used
sharps & capsized spliff
hepatitis rain, a girl
is dancing in it like all

her friends are dead
is how it rains and it rained
all along Lake Shore
that night and all
fucking March
& fucking April, too.

ᓚᕠ

If for one day you
could drive like a car
ad.
If for one night you
could fuck like a
saint.
If the men you did
time with had a mother's
love for
you
or anyone if

this biblical rain
would stop—

Here's to the staggered
Listerine straight
malt-licked two-stepper
in the bikelane
stumbling into the
minuterice-white
jaws of morning

to the plastic bag

the methadone
tomorrow
glow

the kilt-hiking
classcutters,
lipglossed puffs of
vapour & gossip &
the glint & click
of switchblade
manicures

to the hotboxed sedan's
woofer-rending
autotune, KO'd
taillight trailing
skunk

the rap-trilling
babes in arms like
spring fledglings in micro
braids and racing stripes
singing down the sidewalk
with that grade eight
grad swagger

the Eagles-cranking
Harley grinding
that corner again
leathers sweating hot
take it easy
dew

to the ones who never
got away,
squawking acrid
on their nasty old
sofas and their cigarette
stoops

to the bright
trauma of staying
that shines mould-lurid
off every lifer
like a halo

and the burp of siren
launching its pale
headlit
pablum
into the bonyshouldered
night—

& the rain detains
the sky
a little longer

—o here's to that
or any other
light.

Είναι παντού το ποίημα σαν τα φτερά του αγέρα μες
στον αγέρα που άγγιξαν τα φτερά του γλάρου μια στιγμή.

Γιώργος Σεφέρης

ACKNOWLEDGEMENTS

Some of these poems appeared in the *Humber Review, typishly, The Ampersand Review, Southword, Bedfellows, Blue Mountain Review, A Gathering of the Tribes Magazine, Red Fez,* & autoliterate.com. The poem "Bonedog" appeared in Jessie Buckley's mouth in the film *I'm Thinking of Ending Things.*

A very grateful thank you to everyone who helped / housed me: Jan Doherty, MacDowell Arts, Garret Linn, Danny Shot, Chavisa Woods, Charlie Kaufman, Gordon Kipping, Ayelet Waldman, Kok Loong Lye, Martha Baillie, Canisia Lubrin, Bob Hicok, Ayad Akhtar, ac, Chi Nguyen, John Grant Jr, Kim Jennings, Bill & Alan Harnum, the Thorbrooks, the New York Mills Arts Retreat, Michael Dennis, Corin Raymond, Sébastien Jean, Scott Wheeler, Clan Goossen, Jeremiah Brown, Antonio Riva Palacio Lavín, Peter Behrens, Γιώργος Παπαδάτος, Piero Salabè, Nuria Enciso, David Reed, the Communist's Daughter, & the staff and regulars of the Done Right Inn, best arts grant a girl could ask for.

EVA H.D. is the author of *Rotten Perfect Mouth*, *Light Wounds* (with photographer Kendall Townend), and the short film *Jackals & Fireflies*.